The Fireside Book

**A picture and a poem
for every mood
chosen by
David Hope**

Printed and Published by
D. C. THOMSON & CO., LTD.
Dundee and London

MIRACLE

THIS is a miracle to me;
    To see stars shining through a tree;
A tree I planted years ago,
A tiny slip; to see it grow
Until this night I stand below
And lift my eyes to autumn skies,
To branches moving to and fro,
Dropping their burnished leaves, and see
The bright stars shining through my tree.
A miracle that this my hand
Once held this tree 'neath which I stand!

Aileen E. Passmore

A RAINBOW AT CUSHENDALL

THE dark clouds were low over Lurig,
  A rainstorm hid Garron from sight,
When, over the sea from the eastward,
  Gleamed faintly a silvery light,
And, child of the storm and the sunshine
  Love-mingled, a rainbow was born
In beauty that girdled the hill-tops,
  In radiance that lighted the morn;
Its delicate, fairy-spun fabric
  Unfolded its loveliness there,
Filled earth with a breath of enchantment,
  Then faded and vanished in air.

Love, too, has its swift-passing vision,
  Like-fashioned of sorrow and bliss;
Rich, tinted lights, painted by passion,
  Frail beauty conceived in a kiss:
Its glory may live but a moment,
  Its magical colours grow cold,
Yet, kneel at the foot of Love's rainbow,
  And seek for the gleam of its gold.

                                    May Morton

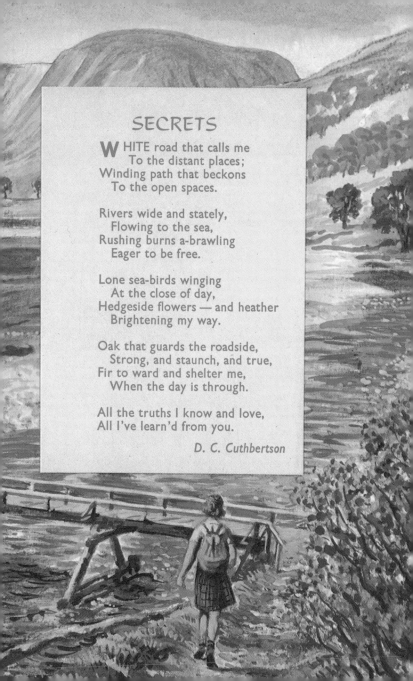

SECRETS

WHITE road that calls me
　　To the distant places;
Winding path that beckons
　　To the open spaces.

Rivers wide and stately,
　　Flowing to the sea,
Rushing burns a-brawling
　　Eager to be free.

Lone sea-birds winging
　　At the close of day,
Hedgeside flowers — and heather
　　Brightening my way.

Oak that guards the roadside,
　　Strong, and staunch, and true,
Fir to ward and shelter me,
　　When the day is through.

All the truths I know and love,
All I've learn'd from you.

D. C. Cuthbertson

THE SAILOR'S WIFE

AND are ye sure the news is true?
   And are ye sure he's weel?
Is this a time to think o' wark?
   Ye jauds, fling bye your wheel!
Is this the time to spin a thread,
   When Colin's at the door?
Rax down my cloak — I'll to the quay,
   And see him come ashore.

   For there's nae luck aboot the house,
      There's nae luck ava;
    There's little pleasure in the house
      When our gudeman's awa'.

And gie to me my bigonet,*   * linen
   My bishop's satin gown;   head-dress
For I maun tell the bailie's wife
   That Colin's in the town.
My Turkey slippers maun gae on,
   My hose o' pearly blue,—
It's a' to pleasure our gudeman,
   For he's baith leal and true.

Rise up and mak' a clean fireside,
　　Put on the muckle pot;
Gie little Kate her button gown,
　　And Jock his Sunday coat;
And mak' their shoon as black as slaes,
　　Their stockin's white as snaw,—
It's a' to please my ain gudeman —
　　He likes to see them braw.

Sae true his heart, sae smooth his speech,
　　His breath like caller* air;　　　*fresh
His very foot has music in't
　　As he comes up the stair.
And will I see his face again?
　　And will I hear him speak?
I'm downright dizzy wi' the thought,—
　　In troth I'm like to greet!*　　*cry

　　For there's nae luck aboot the house,
　　　　There's nae luck ava;
　　There's little pleasure in the house
　　　　When our gudeman's awa'.

W. J. Mickle

THE COTSWOLDS

WHEN God created Gloucestershire,
   I've always understood,
He looked upon His handiwork
   And found that it was good.
He raised our lovely Cotswold Hills
   And, to the Cotswold man,
He gave the wit to carry on
   The work that He began.

He raised our lovely Cotswold Hills
   And saw that they were filled
With lots of lovely Cotswold stone
   That man might also build.
Then, to that first great Architect
   Give praises that are due;
But don't forget that Cotswold men
   Deserve some credit, too.

Reginald Arkell

EAST ANGLIAN BATHE

OH, when the early morning at the seaside
    Took us with hurrying steps from Horsey Mere
To see the whistling bent-grass on the leeside
    And then the tumbled breaker-line appear,
On high, the clouds with mighty adumbration
    Sailed over us to seaward fast and clear
And jellyfish in quivering isolation
    Lay silted in the dry sand of the breeze
And we, along the table-land of beach blown,
    Went gooseflesh from our shoulders to our knees
And ran to catch the football, each to each thrown,
    In the soft and swirling music of the seas.

There splashed about our ankles as we waded
    Those intersecting wavelets morning-cold,
And sudden dark a patch of sea was shaded,
    And sudden light, another patch would hold
The warmth of whirling atoms in a sun-shot
    And underwater sandstorm green and gold.
So in we dived and louder than a gunshot
    Sea-water broke in fountains down the ear.
How cold the bathe, how chattering cold the drying,
    How welcoming the inland reeds appear,
The wood-smoke and the breakfast and the frying,
    And your warm freshwater ripples, Horsey Mere.

John Betjeman

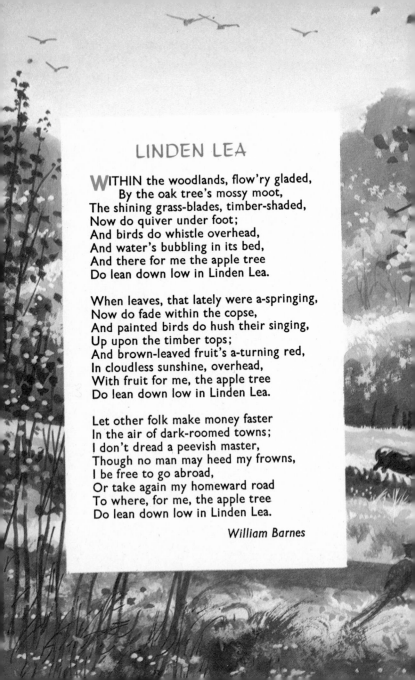

LINDEN LEA

WITHIN the woodlands, flow'ry gladed,
    By the oak tree's mossy moot,
The shining grass-blades, timber-shaded,
Now do quiver under foot;
And birds do whistle overhead,
And water's bubbling in its bed,
And there for me the apple tree
Do lean down low in Linden Lea.

When leaves, that lately were a-springing,
Now do fade within the copse,
And painted birds do hush their singing,
Up upon the timber tops;
And brown-leaved fruit's a-turning red,
In cloudless sunshine, overhead,
With fruit for me, the apple tree
Do lean down low in Linden Lea.

Let other folk make money faster
In the air of dark-roomed towns;
I don't dread a peevish master,
Though no man may heed my frowns,
I be free to go abroad,
Or take again my homeward road
To where, for me, the apple tree
Do lean down low in Linden Lea.

William Barnes

THE SEA LOVER

I CAN smell the sea
  Deep in the Midlands
Amidst the flowers and grass,
The new-cut hay;
Can smell the ocean smell
Of salt and seaweed;
I'd smell them
If a thousand miles away
From surge of sea, and sound
Of white gulls screaming;
Amidst a land-locked country
I would hear
The thunder of the surf
On winter mornings;
Each drift of smoke
Would bring the sea fog near;
Each rainy drop would be the spray
Far-flinging across the rippled sands —
Oh yes, I know
If I were buried under bricks and mortar,
I'd smell the sea and hear the sea winds
    blow!

Aileen E. Passmore

TIME TO GO!

IT'S good to know you're welcome
　When visiting a friend;
　　Compare your news
　　And air your views,
And know it won't offend.

It's good to share the silence
When heart communes with heart,
　　And thought takes wings,
　　The spirit sings,
And doubts and fears depart.

It's good to feel at home there
With one whose ways you know;
　　But the greatest thing,
　　When visiting,
Is knowing when to go!

D. V. Sinclair

THE HEALING BOUGH

IF your friend's ill,
   Bring him a bough:
A branch of the almond
Will best serve him now.
Set it where he can see
The buds on the stem
Open gradually.
He will lie watching them,
Day by day at the first,
And at last hour by hour,
As the deep pink buds burst
Into paler pink flower;
And the changing delight,
And the loveliness, will
Help your friend day and night
While he is ill.
The fruit-tree in season,
The almond-tree now—
If your friend's ill,
Bring him a bough.

Eleanor Farjeon

RIDE A MILE
ON DADDY'S FOOT

RIDE a mile on daddy's foot!
  Up and ride away,
Round and round the stony hill,
  In among the hay.
Out upon the whinny moor,
  Through the windy glen;
Out and in among the trees,
  And through the wood again.

When the moon is full and round
  Fairies play their tricks,
Riding races through the sky
  All upon broomsticks;
Who that has so fleet a horse
  Would not up and ride
Round the world in twenty jumps,
  By the ingleside?

Bonnie bairn, with cheeks so red,
  You have ridden well,
Some day you will have to go
  Through the world yoursel';
Then you'll be a mighty man,
  Tramping on your feet;
May you have a heart as kind,
  And a laugh as sweet.

Robert Bird

IN CITY STREETS

YONDER in the heather there's a bed for
    sleeping,
   Drink for one athirst, ripe blackberries to eat;
Yonder in the sun the merry hares go leaping,
   And the pool is clear for travel-wearied feet.

Sorely throb my feet, a-tramping London highways
   (Ah! the springy moss upon a northern moor!),
Through the endless streets, the gloomy squares
    and byways,
   Homeless in the City, poor among the poor!

London streets are gold—ah, give me leaves
    a-glinting
  'Midst grey dykes and hedges in the autumn sun!
London water's wine, poured out for all unstinting—
  God! For the little brooks that tumble as they
    run!

Oh, my heart is fain to hear the soft wind blowing,
  Soughing through the fir-tops up on northern
    fells!
Oh, my eye's an ache to see the brown burn flowing
  Through the peaty soil and tinkling heather-bells.

Ada Smith

THE GAME THAT'S NEVER DONE

SOFT, soft the sunset falls upon the pitch,
    The game is over and the stumps are drawn,
The willow sleeps in its appointed niche,
The heavy roller waits another dawn—
    Bowled is the final ball again,
    Hushed is the umpire's call again,
The fielders and the batsmen cease to run—
    But memory will play again
    Many and many a day again
The game that's done, the game that's never done.

In happy dreams we'll see each ball re-bowled,
And mend the fault that robbed us of some prize,
In dreams we'll hold the catch we failed to hold,
And see our duck's-eggs swell to centuries—
  In dreams we'll take the field again,
  In dreams the willow wield again,
And set the red ball spinning in the sun—
  Ah, memory will play again
  Many and many a day again
The game that's done, the game that's never done.

Eleanor and Herbert Farjeon

BLOWS THE WIND TODAY

BLOWS the wind today, and the sun and the
    rain are flying,
  Blows the wind on the moors today and now,
Where about the graves of the martyrs the
    whaups* are crying,   * curlews
  My heart remembers how!

Grey recumbent tombs of the dead in desert
    places,
  Standing-stones on the vacant wine-red moor,
Hills of sheep, and the howes of the silent
    vanished races,
  And winds, austere and pure.

Be it granted me to behold you again in dying,
  Hills of home! and to hear again the call;
Hear about the graves of the martyrs the peewees
    crying,
  And hear no more at all.

                    R. L. Stevenson

MY SISTER VISITS ME

SHE wouldn't look behind the doors,
　　Or peep beneath the chairs,
She wouldn't care if there was dust,
　　An inch thick on the stairs.
And yet I clean and fuss about
　　With soap and mopping pail,
Put up new curtains that I got
　　At the last summer sale.

Before she comes I clean the walls,
　　The windows and the doors,
Wash every cupboard in the house,
　　And polish all the floors,
I tidy up the cellar bins
　　Rid out the odds and ends,
And turn the carpet hopefully
　　To try and hide the mends.

And now she's here . . . and all we do
　　Is talk and talk and talk,
We haven't done one thing besides
Since she came from the dock.
She's never even looked to see
　　The house . . . but all the same,
I'm glad I cleaned the corners out,
　　Before my sister came.

Edna Jaques

WINDS

THE South wind brought the smell of country
    things,
New furrows in the sun, and gaudy wings,
Lilies and buttercups beside a pool,
Green pastures growing where the earth is cool.

The West wind brought the salt of stormy seas,
It blew against my face and in the trees,
Made little sounds like children in their sleep,
Bringing to us the stirrings of the deep.

The North wind hissed above the frozen snow,
Bringing vast silence, Northern lights aglow;
Long bitter wastes where stillness reigns complete,
Mocking the little noises of our street.

The East wind brought us fog and gusts of rain,
Beating like hands against the windowpane,
Grey mists and sodden streets and dripping eaves,
Bedraggled flowers in their sheltering leaves.

And when October gales blew cold and high,
We shut the door and let the wind go by;
And turned our backs and pulled the shutters tight,
Glad of warm rooms and shelter from the night.

Edna Jaques

SPRING

EVERY sweet bud unfolding,
   Every green leaf unfurled
For the joy of man's beholding,
   In God's most wonderful world.

Every small star bright shining,
   Every soft breeze astir,
All nature's heart enshrining
   His beauty everywhere.

Every strong shoot upsurging,
   Every cold drop of rain
Blessing new life emerging,
   As spring comes round again.

Aileen E. Passmore

OVER THE HILLS
AND FAR AWAY

WHERE forlorn sunsets flare and fade
  On desolate sea and lonely sand,
Out of the silence and the shade
  What is the voice of strange command
Calling you still, as friend calls friend,
  With love that cannot brook delay,
To rise and follow the ways that wend
  Over the hills and far away?

Hark in the city, street on street
  A roaring reach of death and life,
Of vortices that clash and fleet
  And ruin in appointed strife,
Hark to it calling, calling clear,
  Calling until you cannot stay
From dearer things than your own most dear
  Over the hills and far away.

Out of the sound of the ebb-and-flow,
　　Out of the sight of lamp and star,
It calls you where the good winds blow,
　　And the unchanging meadows are:
From faded hopes and hopes agleam,
　　It calls you, calls you night and day
Beyond the dark into the dream
　　Over the hills and far away.

W. E. Henley

THE NEST

A THREAD of wool from the fold,
  From the pond a beakful of clay,
Twisted and beaten and rolled
  In love's own wonderful way:
We have twined it and woven it warm and neat
And the April winds may gather and beat,
But the slender walls of our home shall hold
  The winds of the world at bay.

A splash of blue from the sky,
  A fleck of brown from the mould,
And our four bright jewels lie
  In my warm wing's circling fold;
I have wrapped them close in my bosom-heat,
I have turned them under my tiny feet,
And, shielded safe as the showers go by,
  Have covered from all Earth's cold.

With the green on the budding thorn,
  With the white on the apple tree,
Shall our nestlings four be born
  And our first watch ended be;
I shall feel them moving warm at my feet,
With their mute mouths opened to mine for
    meat,
While a brown bird up with the early morn
  Brings his loot of the lawn to me.

Will H. Ogilvie

IN NATURE'S GARDEN

IT is the hour when from the boughs
  The nightingale's high note is heard;
It is the hour when lovers' vows
Seem sweet in every whispered word;
And gentle winds, and waters near,
Make music to the lonely ear.
Each flower the dews have lightly wet,
And in the sky the stars are met,
And on the wave is deeper blue,
And on the leaf a browner hue,
And in the heaven that clear obscure,
So softly dark, and darkly pure,
Which follows the decline of day,
As twilight melts beneath the moon away.

Byron

THE SKATERS

HOW fancy paints that bygone day
  When you were here, my fair—
The whole lake rang with rapid skates
  In the windless, winter air.

You leaned to me, I leaned to you,
  Our course was smooth as flight —
We steered — a heel-touch to the left,
  A heel-touch to the right.

We swung our way through flying men,
  Your hand lay fast in mine,
We saw the shifting crowd dispart,
  The level ice-reach shine.

I swear by yon swan-travelled lake,
  By yon calm hill above,
I swear had we been drowned that day
  We had been drowned in love.

R. L. Stevenson

LULLABY

THE rooks' nests do rock on the tree-top,
  Where few foes can stand;
The martin's is high and is deep
  In the steep clift of sand;
But thou, love, a-sleeping where footsteps
  Might come to thy bed,
Hast father and mother to watch thee
  And shelter thy head.
     Lullaby, Lilybrow, lie asleep;
     Blest be thy rest.

And some birds do keep under roofing
  Their young from the storm;
And some wi' nest-hoodings o' moss
  And o' wool, do lie warm.
And we will look well to the house-roof
  That o'er thee might leak,
And the beast that might beat on thy window
  Shall not smite thy cheek.
     Lullaby, Lilybrow, lie asleep;
     Blest be thy rest.

William Barnes

A SONG OF THE FOUR SEASONS

WHEN Spring comes laughing
　　By vale and hill,
By wind-flower walking
　　And daffodil,—
Sing stars of morning,
　　Sing morning skies,
Sing blue of speedwell,—
　　And my Love's eyes.

When comes the Summer,
　　Full-leaved and strong,
And gay birds gossip
　　The orchard long,—
Sing hid, sweet honey
　　That no bee sips;
Sing red, red roses,—
　　And my Love's lips.

When Autumn scatters
　　The leaves again,
And piled sheaves bury
　　The broad-wheeled wain,—
Sing flutes of harvest
　　Where men rejoice;
Sing rounds of reapers,—
　　And my Love's voice.

But when comes Winter
　　With hail and storm,
And red fire roaring
　　And ingle warm,—
Sing first sad going
　　Of friends that part;
Then sing glad meeting,—
　　And my Love's heart.

Austin Dobson

CAMBRIDGE

WHEN we are gone and this bright sun
    Shines into other eyes,
This ageless river still shall run
Beneath the Cambridge skies.

The leafy dawns will still awake
Beyond the climbing spires;
The chiming bells at evening take
All dreams and all desires.

Each ancient college, church and street,
This courtyard lit with flowers
Will hear the sound of other feet
And other words than ours.

This singing city that can move
Our hearts with joy, must be
Seen only through love's eyes to prove
Its immortality.

Douglas Gibson

THE PEACE OF GOD AND MEN

GOD'S peace to me, peace of mankind,
    And Saint Columba's peace, the kind,
Mild Mary's peace, a loving thing,
And peace of Christ the tender King,
    The peace of Christ the tender King,

Be on each window, on each door,
Each cranny-light upon the floor,
On house four corners may it fall,
And on my bed's four corners all,
    Upon my bed's four corners all;

Upon each thing mine eye doth see,
Upon each food that enters me,
Upon my body of the earth,
And on my soul of heavenly birth,
    Upon my body of the earth,
    Upon my soul of heavenly birth.

Translated from the Gaelic by
G. R. D. MacLean

FRIENDLY RIVALS

I KNOW that I'm no wizard
   Of skill upon the rink,
But bowling's made for friendship—
   And that's the way I think.

I'm happy if I win a match,
   Still happy if I lose,
If only I am playing
   Among the friends I choose.

Give me a summer evening,
  When work is left behind,
When the sun is on the poplars,
  The breeze comes soft and kind—

I wouldn't swop my pleasure
  With princes or with kings,
For how could they be knowing
  The friendship bowling brings?

David Hope

OLD CRACKED PLATE

IT isn't only an old cracked plate
   With roses around the brim,
There is something else that you cannot name
   In the pattern old and dim;
A little tie with the past that clings
   Like a lovely perfume to older things.

For my grandmother told me when I was small
    That it came from across the sea
In a sailing ship with a golden prow
    In eighteen thirty-three,
And her mother before her had used the plate
    For the special feasts and the days of state.

A bit of sentiment, yes, I know,
    From a heart long dead and the past,
And a seacoast village below the cliffs
    And a ship with a broken mast,
Where sailors walk in their hodden blue
    And dream of a ship with a Yorkshire crew.

So, you see, it's more than a china plate
    With roses and scroll work on;
It is faith and love and a hope that lives
    When a race of men are gone;
A tie like a golden chain to hold
    This brave today with the days of old.

Edna Jaques

TO A HAPPY PERSON

POUR me laughter in a brimming rummer
　　of sparkling joy, and I shall live again,
basking in all the radiant warmth of summer
　　whatever winters chill less lucky men;
now, in your cheerful eye and dimpled cheek,
　　I taste encouragement divinely sent,
and, having tasted, need no longer seek
　　reason to live. You are my argument.

Oh God forbid that any doubting frown
　　should crease your brow, implanted there by
　　　me.
or your brave shoulders ever be bowed down
　　with the least ounce of folly's misery.
Give me your pack. Your laugh is of that sort
which makes an extra mile seem all too short.

Kiss me, my sweet, and with your kiss lift half
　　the burden of my care away; and then
remove the other portion with your laugh,
　　bringing the Golden Age back to my ken —
the age when Adam never thought it odd
to walk in Eden and to laugh with God.

Philip Stalker

THE LINK

I HAVE come to the time when I often think
   Of the ones I used to know,
And their happy voices reach down the years
   With the warmth of afterglow.

There are some who have gone to those Mansions
    bright,
   At the end of their quiet sleeping;
But their daily love, and their unsung deeds,
   Stay unblemished in my keeping.

Others there are who have crossed the sea,
   Or travelled beyond my knowing;
They have left me lost as the dry, dead leaves
   In the winds of autumn blowing.

The relentless grandeur of passing days
   At last shall all ties sever,
But those who were young when I was young
   Live on in my heart for ever.

Margaret Bentley

WASHING UP

HOW shall we sing of the washing of dishes?
    What shall we tell of the drying of plates?
What of the food that at simplest and plainest
Hideous holocaust ever creates?
What of the sink-side that bends 'neath a burden,
Staggering skyward in piles as it waits?
              Sisters, fear not!
              Water is hot.

What shall we tell of the rinsing of glasses?
Threads from the cloth that with steady adherence
Teach us more truly than Bruce and his spider
High is the value of true perseverance,
What of the cutlery, spiteful and tangled,
Sticky in contact and stained in appearance?
              Sisters, have hope!
              Here is the soap.

How shall we mourn for the rent-riven teapot
Dealt its last death-blow against the hot tap?
How shall we weep for the best cup and saucer
Parting so softly beneath a slight rap?
What of the milk-jugs that plunge to destruction,
Plates that disintegrate, handles that snap?
              Sisters, no tear!
              Woolworths is near.

Let us sing rather of scintillant saucepans,
Mirror-like metal, and glittering glass,
Covers wherein an unflattering version
Of figure and features appears as we pass,
Porcelain pellucid and pure as the snowdrift,
Shimmer of steel and brilliance of brass.
              Come, sisters, drat it!
              Up, mops, and at it!

                                    Molly Capes

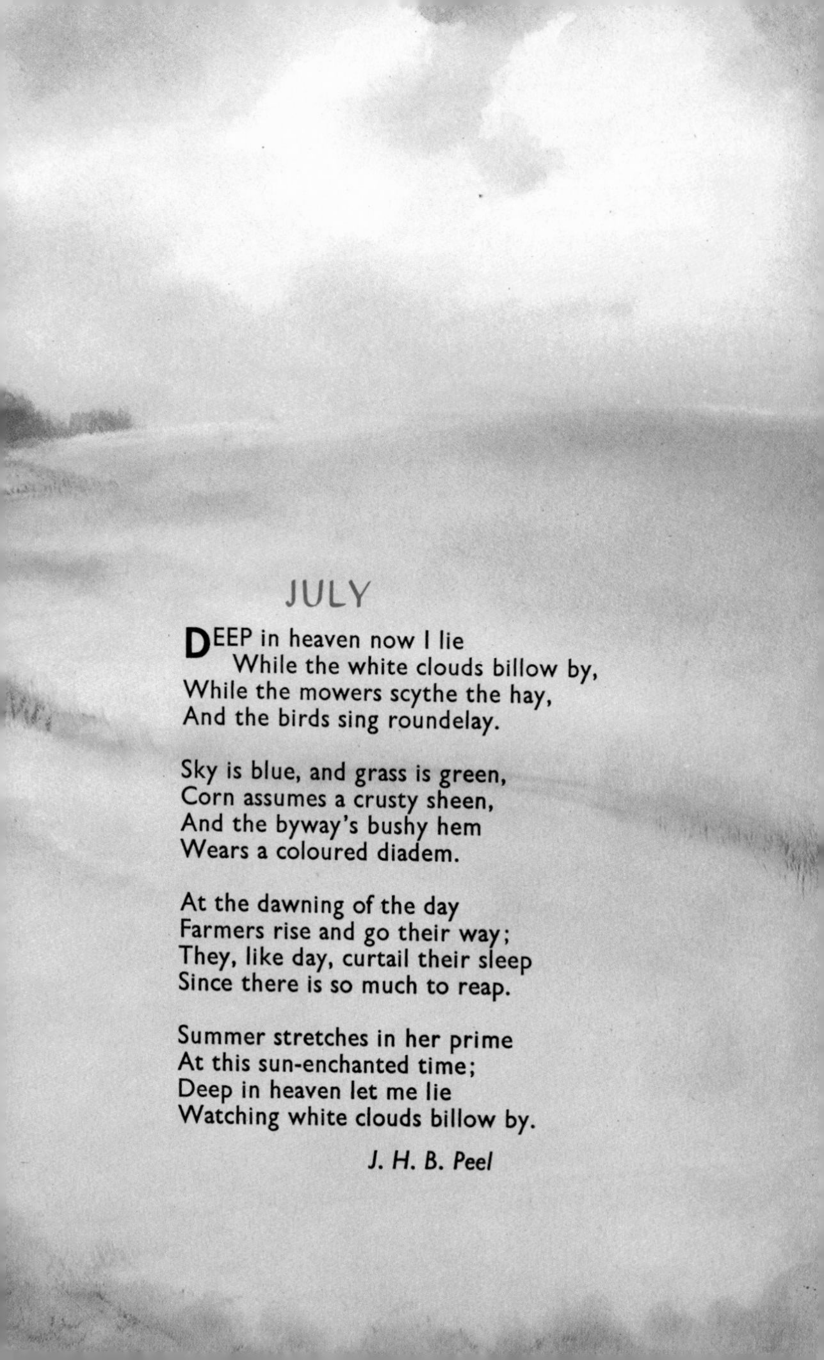

JULY

DEEP in heaven now I lie
    While the white clouds billow by,
While the mowers scythe the hay,
And the birds sing roundelay.

Sky is blue, and grass is green,
Corn assumes a crusty sheen,
And the byway's bushy hem
Wears a coloured diadem.

At the dawning of the day
Farmers rise and go their way;
They, like day, curtail their sleep
Since there is so much to reap.

Summer stretches in her prime
At this sun-enchanted time;
Deep in heaven let me lie
Watching white clouds billow by.

J. H. B. Peel

SHIPS

YOU ask me why I wander so?
   I cannot tell you why;
You'll have to blame it on the stars
   And on the wind and sky.
Today I heard a silver song
   And saw a ship go by.

A hundred voices on the air
   That mock my quiet day,
Salt winds that whisper to my heart,
   Such happy tunes they play,
So I must gather up my tools
   And follow them away.

If I should live in little towns
   That do not know the sea,
But only pastures green and still
   Where cattle love to be,
I might forget the winding roads
   That call and call to me.

Beyond the sea the sun went down
   And left a golden sky,
So I went out to see the ships
   And hear the seagulls cry;
But when I saw their swinging masts
   I could not say goodbye.

Edna Jaques

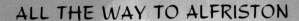

ALL THE WAY TO ALFRISTON

ALL the way to Alfriston,
   From Chichester to Alfriston,
I went along the running Downs
High above the patchwork plain,
Fantastical as Joseph's coat
With coloured squares of grass and grain,
Earthen russets, duns and browns,
Charlock-yellow, clover-green,
Reddening wheat and silvery oat:
And rivers coiling in between,
And roofs of little peopled towns.

I heard the wind among the leaves
And corn that was not yet in sheaves
Swishing with the sound of surf;
I heard the cry of distant trains,
The rush and drip of scudding rains,
I heard my foot-beat on the turf,
The lark's delight, the peewit's plaint,
Hoarse calls of shepherds, bark and bleat,
Sheep-bells and church-bells in the heat,
And rambling thunders, far and faint;
And I saw dew-ponds round as pearls,
And multitudes of summer flowers,
Mulleins tall as little girls,
And Canterbury bells in showers.

I ate my bread in open places,
I changed a smile with many faces,
I loved the jokes and commerce with
The jolly baker and the smith,
The gipsy with her wheedling eyes,
Her pack of wares, her pack of lies;
I loved the rain-storms and the sun,
The silent shepherds young and old,
I loved the cropping, wandering fold,
The silky dog that chased the sheep,
I loved my rest when day was done,
I loved the Downs, awake, asleep,
All the way to Alfriston,
From Chichester to Alfriston.

Eleanor Farjeon

PICTURES ON THE WINDOW

WHEN the frost is on the orchard
   And inside the fire glows,
That's the time to make your picture,
   As every artist knows.

You can draw a fleet of warships,
   Or a quite enormous train,
A horse and knight in armour
   And a super dock-side crane.

Daddy says it's " messy,"
   But he doesn't mind a lot;
When he thought I wasn't watching,
   I saw him have a shot!

David Hope

THE FIDDLER OF DOONEY

WHEN I play on my fiddle in Dooney
    Folk dance like a wave of the sea;
My cousin is priest in Kilvarnet,
My brother in Moharabuiee.

I pass'd my brother and cousin:
They read in their books of prayer;
I read in my book of songs
I bought at the Sligo fair.

When we come at the end of time,
To Peter sitting in state,
He will smile on the three old spirits,
But call me first through the gate;

For the good are always the merry,
Save by an evil chance;
And the merry love the fiddle,
And the merry love to dance:

And when the folk there spy me,
They will all come up to me,
With " Here is the fiddler of Dooney!"
And dance like a wave of the sea.

W. B. Yeats

SEASIDE MORNING

A SOLITARY gull walks
  delicately on stilts
at the shore's edge
where the quiet waves crinkle
the sugary sand.

The sea is blue silk
with scarcely a wrinkle,
and the small boats stand
on their own reflections;
the white sails tremble.

I walk in a secret world
like the gull this autumn morning,
tasting the salty air
and the apricot's sun perfection,
exulting in the softness
of the sand under my feet,
and the firm ribbed lines
that the waves have carved.

I found
garlands of green seaweed
and this white stone
beautiful and smooth as an egg
veined with gold-brown:
souvenirs of the morning
to take home.

Douglas Gibson

THE EXPLANATION

OLD Silas Griggs, the gardener,
    Was sitting in the sun,
Telling his little daughter
    All the things that he had done.
Of how he helped to build the Ark,
    And Silas told her, too,
Of Adam and the Apple,
    And the Garden where it Grew.
" There was a woman," Silas said,
    " And her I chiefly blames,
She started calling everything
    By all them Latin names.
The Master couldn't understand
    What it was all about;
And so he sends an Angel down,
    And turns poor Adam out.
Some people sez as he was wrong,
    But I sez he was right,
'Tis all these filthy foreign names
    As brings in all the blight.
And anyone, with any sense,
    Is certain to agree
That English names for English flowers
    Is good enough for we."

Reginald Arkell

VALERIAN

I KNOW the scented hills of Grasse,
  The gentians of an Alpine pass,
Wild thyme upon a Sussex down,
The tulip fields of Haarlem Town.

I've seen wistaria by the Seine,
Wild roses in a Wiltshire lane;
I've paddled in a sea of blue,
When it was bluebell time at Kew.

I know the smell of burning peat,
And meadows full of meadow-sweet;
The coral foam of apple trees—
But though I think of all of these,

Valerian, on a Cotswold wall,
Is what I like the best of all.

Reginald Arkell

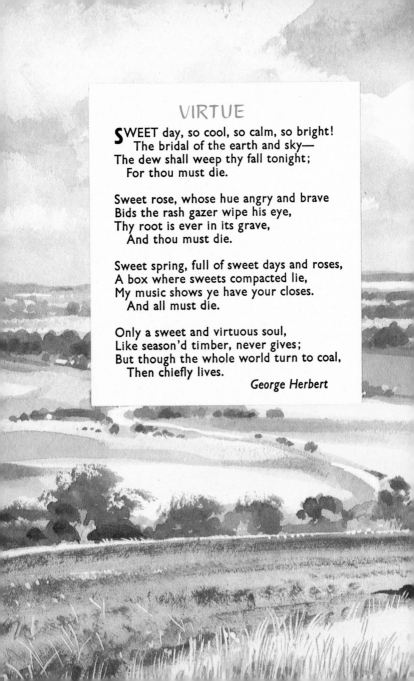

VIRTUE

SWEET day, so cool, so calm, so bright!
  The bridal of the earth and sky—
The dew shall weep thy fall tonight;
  For thou must die.

Sweet rose, whose hue angry and brave
Bids the rash gazer wipe his eye,
Thy root is ever in its grave,
  And thou must die.

Sweet spring, full of sweet days and roses,
A box where sweets compacted lie,
My music shows ye have your closes.
  And all must die.

Only a sweet and virtuous soul,
Like season'd timber, never gives;
But though the whole world turn to coal,
  Then chiefly lives.

George Herbert

THE LAST APPLES

THE air is cold, the sky is grey,
　　No sunlight warms the winter day;
In the wet garden a bird grieves
For faded flowers and fallen leaves.
But the last apples on the trees
From leafless boughs shine brilliantly,
More red than any robin's breast
Or sunset at its crimson crest.

I pluck the apples, one by one,
The fruit of a remembered sun
That from our shelves will gaily shine
All through the winter, warm as wine:
In smell and flavour unsurpassed
Are apples we have left till last.

Douglas Gibson

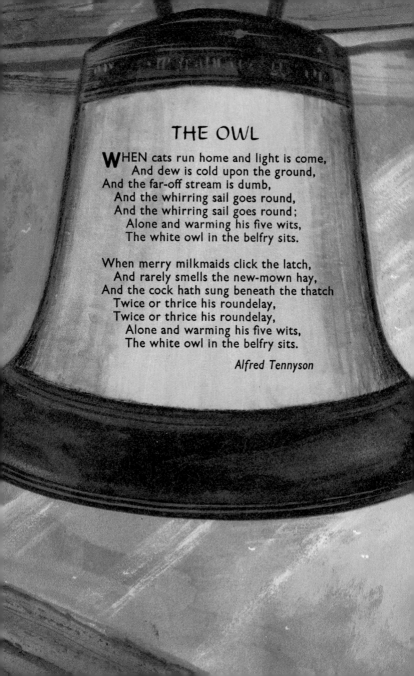

THE OWL

WHEN cats run home and light is come,
    And dew is cold upon the ground,
And the far-off stream is dumb,
    And the whirring sail goes round,
    And the whirring sail goes round;
      Alone and warming his five wits,
      The white owl in the belfry sits.

When merry milkmaids click the latch,
    And rarely smells the new-mown hay,
And the cock hath sung beneath the thatch
    Twice or thrice his roundelay,
    Twice or thrice his roundelay,
      Alone and warming his five wits,
      The white owl in the belfry sits.

Alfred Tennyson

DOUN THE BURN

WHEN trees did bud, and fields were green,
And broom bloom'd fair to see;
When Mary was complete fifteen,
And love laugh'd in her e'e;
Blythe Davie's blinks her heart did move
To speak her mind thus free:
Gang doun the burn, Davie, love,
And I will follow thee!

Now Davie did each lad surpass
 That dwelt on this burnside;
And Mary was the bonniest lass,
 Just meet to be a bride:
Her cheeks were rosy-red and white,
 Her e'en were bonnie blue,
Her looks were like Aurora bright,
 Her lips like dropping dew.

What pass'd, I guess, was harmless play,
 And naething sure unmeet;
For, ganging hame, I heard them say
 They liked a walk sae sweet,
And that they aften should return
 Sic pleasure to renew.
Quoth Mary, Love, I like the burn,
 And aye shall follow you!

Robert Crawford

OXFORD

I CAME to Oxford in the light
   Of a spring-coloured afternoon;
Some clouds were grey and some were white,
   And all were blown to such a tune
Of quiet rapture in the sky,
I laughed to see them laughing by.

I had been dreaming in the train
   With thoughts at random from my book;
I looked, and read, and looked again,
   And suddenly to greet my look
Oxford shone up with every tower
Aspiring sweetly like a flower.

Home turn the feet of men that seek,
   And home the hearts of children turn,
And none can teach the hour to speak
   What every hour is free to learn;
And all discover, late or soon,
Their golden Oxford afternoon.

Gerald Gould

AGAIN

AIN'T it good to see again
   Leaf an' bud an' bee again —
Friends a fellow knows!
Ain't it good to feel again
Hook an' rod an' reel again
   Where the ripple flows!
Ain't it grand to hear again
Larks a-singing clear again
To know the summer's near again
   An' pinnin' on her rose!

Ain't it good to find again
Winter's left behind again,
   Summer's ridin' in.
Ain't it good to pass again
Blue things in the grass again,
   Gold things on the whin!
Ain't it sweet to smell again
South winds off the fell again
Sailin' in to tell again
   Tales of where they've bin!

Ain't it rare to rove again
Through the light an' love again
   The colour an' the call!
Ain't it good to take again
Life for life's own sake again,
   Lettin' trouble fall!
Ain't it grand to know again
Seasons come an' go again,
Spring tides ebb an' flow again,
   An' God is over all!

Will H. Ogilvie

A THREE-PART SONG

I'M just in love with all these three,
  The Weald and the Marsh and the
Down countree.
Nor I don't know which I love the most,
The Weald or the Marsh or the white
                      Chalk coast!

I've buried my heart in a ferny hill,
Twix' a liddle low shaw an' a great high gill.
Oh hop-bine yaller an' wood-smoke blue,
I reckon you'll keep her middling true!

I've loosed my mind for to out and run
On a Marsh that was old when Kings begun.
Oh Romney Level and Brenzett reeds,
I reckon you know what my mind needs!

I've given my soul to the Southdown grass,
And sheep-bells tinkled where you pass.
Oh Firle an' Ditchling an' sails at sea,
I reckon you keep my soul for me!

Rudyard Kipling

TO A FISH OF THE BROOK

WHY flyest thou away with fear?
    Trust me there's naught of danger near,
  I have no wicked hook,
All covered with a snaring bait,
Alas, to tempt thee to thy fate,
  And drag thee from the brook.

Enjoy thy stream, O harmless fish;
And when an angler for his dish,
  Through gluttony's vile sin,
Attempts, a wretch, to pull thee out,
God give thee strength, O gentle trout,
  To pull the rascal in!

John Walcot

THE LITTLE WAVES OF BREFFNY

THE grand road from the mountain goes shining
   to the sea,
  And there is traffic in it, and many a horse and
    cart;
But the little roads of Cloonagh are dearer far to me,
  And the little roads of Cloonagh go rambling
    through my heart.

A great storm from the ocean goes shouting o'er
   the hill,
  And there is glory in it and terror on the wind;
But the haunted air of twilight is very strange and
   still,
  And the little winds of twilight are dearer to my
    mind.

The great waves of the Atlantic sweep storming on
   their way,
  Shining green and silver with the hidden herring
    shoal;
But the Little Waves of Breffny have drenched my
   heart in spray,
  And the Little Waves of Breffny go stumbling
    through my soul.

Eva Gore-Booth

THE BELLS OF YOUTH

THE Bells of Youth are ringing in the gateways
    of the South;
    The bannerets of green are now unfurled;
Spring has risen with a laugh, a wild-rose in her
    mouth,
    And is singing, singing, singing thro' the world.

The Bells of Youth are ringing in all the silent places,
    The primrose and the celandine are out:
Children run a-laughing with joy upon their faces,
    The west wind follows after with a shout.

The Bells of Youth are ringing from the forests to
    the mountains,
    From the meadows to the moorlands, hark their
        ringing!
Ten thousand thousand splashing rills and fern-
    dappled fountains
    Are flinging wide the Song of Youth, and onward
        flowing, singing!

The Bells of Youth are ringing in the gateways of
    the South:
    The bannerets of green are now unfurled:
Spring has risen with a laugh, a wild-rose in her
    mouth,
    And is singing, singing, singing thro' the world.

" *Fiona Macleod* " (*William Sharp*)

ONLY SLEEPING

NOT every ghost is sad:
    Some ghosts leave laughter,
Echoes of happy days
And sun-filled hours,
For any heedless heart
Can be contented
When all the world
Is gay with summer flowers.
It takes a keener mind
To smile on winter,
Braving the coldness
And the stinging rain,
So gather up the rags
Of last year's dreaming,
Banish your sorrow
And begin again.

Margaret Bentley

FISHING FROM THE PIER

THERE'S folk that find their joy in flight,
    And folk that mountaineer;
Some go bird-watching through the night
    And some will stalk a deer.
For all these pleasures, big and small,
    I wouldn't shed a tear;
The chiefest joy I can recall
    Is fishing from the pier!

Some do it with a line and hook,
  Some do it with a pin;
Some have flies and proper bait,
  Or earthworms in a tin;
It's all the same what bait you get
  When dabs or skate are near;
A worm'll bring you no regret
  When fishing from the pier!

The pleasure's not the fish you catch,
  It's not the skill you show;
This ploy is endless glamour
  Which only laddies know.
For all life's pleasures, big or small
  I wouldn't shed a tear,
The chiefest joy I can recall
  Is fishing from the pier!

D. Dunbar

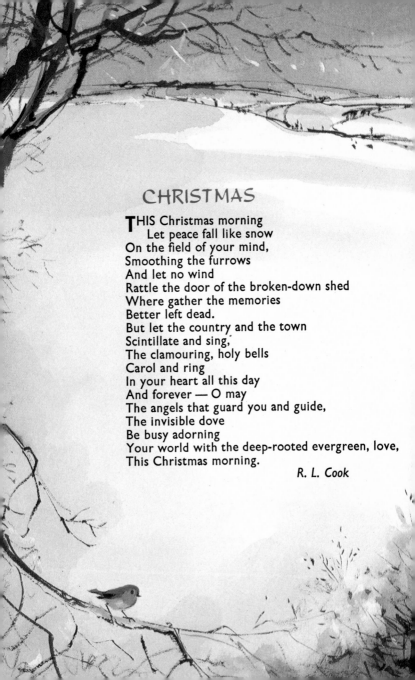

CHRISTMAS

THIS Christmas morning
   Let peace fall like snow
On the field of your mind,
Smoothing the furrows
And let no wind
Rattle the door of the broken-down shed
Where gather the memories
Better left dead.
But let the country and the town
Scintillate and sing,
The clamouring, holy bells
Carol and ring
In your heart all this day
And forever — O may
The angels that guard you and guide,
The invisible dove
Be busy adorning
Your world with the deep-rooted evergreen, love,
This Christmas morning.

R. L. Cook

THANK YOU

THANK you for being just the way you are,
    For eyes that shine — lips that say happy
    things,
For sudden laughter at a foolish joke,
    The joy and comfort that your presence brings.

Thank you — for wood piled up beside the hearth,
    For homey chores performed with willing grace,
The cellar cleaned, the yard kept neat and nice,
    And all the little jobs about the place.

Thank you — for fireglow and little rooms,
    Companionship and all that it implies,
Reading our books together by the fire,
    The look of happy comfort in your eyes.

For tears and gladness . . . faith and trust and
    love,
    Storm clouds and that bright glimmer of a star,
Through all we've shared together down the years,
    Thank you for being just the way you are.

Edna Jaques

ACKNOWLEDGMENTS

To Herbert Jenkins and Barrie & Jenkins for "The Cotswolds," "The Explanation" and "Valerian" by Reginald Arkell: to John Murray for "East Anglian Bathe" by John Betjeman: to Collins for "The Healing Bough" and "All The Way To Alfriston" by Eleanor Farjeon, and "The Game That's Never Done" by Eleanor and Herbert Farjeon: to Mr George Ogilvie and Miss Wendy Ogilvie for "The Nest" and "Again" by Will H. Ogilvie: to S.P.C.K. for G. R. D. MacLean's translation of "The Peace of God and Men": to the Ramsay Head Press for "To A Happy Person" by Philip Stalker: to George G. Harrap for "Washing Up" by Molly Capes: to Donald Copeman for "July" by J. H. B. Peel: to M. B. Yeats, Miss Anne Yeats and Macmillan of London and Basingstoke for "The Fiddler of Dooney" by W. B. Yeats: to Mrs George Bambridge and Macmillan for "A Three-Part Song" by Rudyard Kipling: to The Longman Group Ltd. for "The Little Waves of Breffny" by Eva Gore-Booth.